# THE OUIJA BOARD

## CONTACTING THE DEAD, DANGERS AND DEMONS

M .CRYPTKEEPER

ISBN: 1545559198

ISBN-13: 978-1545559192

# CONTENTS

# THE HiSTORY OF OUiJA BOARDS, WHERE DiD THEY COME FROM?

The Ouija board is a tool used to contact spirits.
They are rectangular in shape and are usually made from wood (or any other smooth/sturdy material). It's a board with letters, numbers and other signs around it. This involves the words: "Yes", "No" and "Goodbye". The numbers 0 – 9 and the full alphabet A – Z.
A planchette is use to supposedly answer questions asked during a séance.

The word Ouija is a combination of the two words: "oui" and "ja" which mean "yes" (in both French and German).

February 1891 - The first few advertisements for this tool started appearing (in various papers) they read:
"Ouija, the Wonderful Talking Board."
These boards were vended from a Pittsburgh toy shop they guaranteed a strong link

"between the known and unknown, the material and immaterial."
News spread about this trend and the Ouija craze spread to New York and beyond.

The real history of the Ouija board is still largely a mystery. It's almost as mysterious as how the board actually works.
Well known Ouija historian: Robert Murch has been researching the origins of the board since 1992.
When Murch began his research, he said, no one knew anything about its origins. This was odd to him: "For such an iconic thing that strikes both fear and wonder in American culture, how can no one know where it came from?"
Most say The Ouija board was born in response to the American 19th century obsession with spiritualism - with the added desire to communicate with the dead, as part of the living.

Spiritualism had been prominent for years in Europe but its popularity grew massively in America in 1848. Spiritualism worked for Americans: it was mostly compatible with Christian beliefs. However in recent years there's been a huge "demonic" association related to Ouija boards, due to incorrect portrayals in horror movies and alternative cultures. Therefore its usage has been denounced in most Christian groups/practices.

The movement offered comfort in an era when the average lifespan was under 50 years old (unlike today). Women died mostly in childbirth; children died of diseases/illness and men died in combat (due to wars). Even well-known figures in history used the Ouija board. One of the most touching séances were those of Mary Todd Lincoln (wife of the American president), who conducted séances in the White House after her son died from a fever in 1862; he was only 11 years old.

Another example of its purpose was shown during the Civil War. People were desperate to connect with loved ones who'd gone away to war and hadn't returned home. It gave children and adults closure. More importantly it allowed an escape from the traumas of the world during sessions.

# THE PLANCHETTE

A planchette is French for "little plank". These tools are usually made of wood are small in size and are heart shaped. Planchettes are key to connecting with entities.

Paranormal investigators and mystics believe the planchette is moved by the energy of spirits. When using one you place your finger on the planchette with no hard force (it should just barely touch) the spirit you've contacted will then surge its energy into it, allowing it to move and allow it to communicate via Ouija board .While others are skeptical and believe it due to a the ideomotor effect.

*The ideomotor effect: A psychological phenomenon where the subject makes motions/movements unconsciously. This involves automatic writing, dowsing and facilitated communication.*

# DO OUIJA BOARDS WORK?

The Ouija board is an extremely useful tool for individuals that desire to gather knowledge from the spirit realm. With patience, practice and respectful behavior this mystical divination tool can awaken your natural psychic ability. A small percentage of people who use Ouija boards don't follow the correct procedures and can gather unresponsive activity. With study and practice many have experienced interactions with deceased loved ones, who have given extremely intimate details in their responses. Others have banished unwanted spirits from certain dwellings and also brought positive energies closer to them.

To answer the question do they actually work? It depends on you as an individual.

Many believe the Ouija reflects the state of mind of the individuals who are using it (on a subconscious level). If you're nervous, scared or expecting something negative to happen, that's the reaction you might get. If you don't believe in the spirit world or come into the experience with doubt then the board will most likely not work on you.

On the other hand, usually people using it with the complete opposite attitude have had very positive experiences and the board works as intended (instead of being a failed session).

# DANGERS WHEN USING THE OUIJA BOARD? WHAT TO AVOID

THE OUJIA BOARD IS NOT A TOY! Contacting spirits comes with a heavy responsibility. Personally I wouldn't recommend using an Ouija board with/in the vicinity of immature beings. In response to children using this tool - personally I believe it has too many risks. If your child or younger friend/relative persists in using one make sure they understand the implications and ask for parental consent when necessary.

There are also many other dangers the following points are things you should avoid performing around this device.

- NEVER participate or even be present around the board under the influence of alcohol/drugs (this doesn't exclude others in your selected group).

- Anyone that is sick, depressed, nervous, stressed etc. should not participate too, as they can draw in a lower vibration spirit or dark energy.

- Do not use the Ouija board by yourself. Have a circle of like-minded people to assist you.

- Do not confuse the spirit(s) with questions from too many people. Assign one person in the room to ask questions (if needed you can switch over; notify the spirit(s) to tie up any loose ends from the original question leader).

- Do not ask questions you don't want to know the answer to. For example: "When am I going to die?" or ask for advice regarding medical/health or relationships. Keep your personal affairs away from spirits, as they can manipulate your energy by giving false/untrustworthy answers – Never open yourself up to potentially powerful or dark forces.

- Do not ask questions you already know the answer to. For example "What is my middle name?" Take the séance seriously. You are meant to be gaining knowledge about the spirit realm, not antagonizing or belittling the spirit with personal pop quiz questions.

- Do not allow the invited spirit guest to control the session. Make the majority of your questions open ended and don't allow them to probe or lecture. Creating boundaries is key. Start the session by expressing how you would prefer the entity to behave and what you want out of the experience.

- Don't ask for physical signs: this is something that is always shown in the majority of horror/supernatural movies. However this can be extremely dangerous, during a session the veil between here and the spirit world is at its thinnest. Poltergeist activity can pass on negative energy within your atmosphere or the surfaces/objects that are tampered with by the spirit.

- Don't lose power or control over the session. If the board starts being rude, aggressive or using obscene language and negative responses – for example the spirit/entity sends the message of "LEAVE!" or "GET OUT!" immediately break off the session by closing the board correctly (as shown in chapter). Rarely you may come in contact with demons (more intricate warning signs and demon names can be found in the following chapter).

- Don't close the board incorrectly. You need to break ties and release any spiritual connections (positive or negative) that is holding onto yourself and the surrounding area.

# STEP BY STEP HOW TO USE A OUiJA BOARD - IN TEN EASY POiNTS

Before following these instructions please match your séance area.
Use the board at night, as less interference is in the atmosphere. However you can use it anytime.
Darken the room and light some candles (white candles). Turn any music or technology off to minimize distractions and unnecessary noise.

Now you can begin:

1. Gather your participants – form a circle as this will build a safe space to begin contact.

2. Assign the position of question asker (as referenced in the previous chapter: too many people asking questions can

confuse spirits – refer back to this section for more information).

3. Clean the board/cleanse the area (if needed) this will also be the perfect time to light any white candles (as advised previously).

4. Perform an opening prayer/chant (optional but this is STRONGLY advised, as a sign of respect).

5. Everyone place one finger on the planchette – Don't push down hard it needs no force your finger should allow the planchette to move freely when the spirit conducts it.

6. Clearly state your intentions to the spirit world and introduce the group.

7. Show the spirit where hello and goodbye are. Trace the planchette around the board a few times allowing the spirit to acknowledge the letters and numbers they will be using – talk them through this process as they may be unsure how to use this form of communication.

8. Ask your first question: "What is your name?" is always a great place to start. Focus and wait for the planchette to move. Keep track of the letters/numbers being selected. Note them down if desired by your designated scribe (if you have one). Keep asking your questions.

9. When the group is finished, or is asked to stop by the spirit (or the energy is negative). Move the planchette to the word "GOODBYE" while saying your thanks, as a mark of respect. Flip the

planchette and place the pointer away from the board.

10. End with a closing prayer or chant – cleanse again if needed. Flip the board and allow it to settle in the area for a brief time, to allow all built up activity/energy to dissipate.

## OPENING PRAYERS/CHANTS OF PROTECTION

Ouija opening prayers/chants are performed before at the start of the session (timing for these prayers/chants can be found in the 10 step guide) it's a great way to open the session with positive energy.

You can use these prayers/chants, or make your own.

- *The Lord is my shepherd, I shall not want.
  He makes me to lie down in green pastures;
  he leads me beside the still waters. He
  restores my soul. He guides me in the paths
  of righteousness for his name's sake. Even
  though I walk through the valley of the
  shadow of death, I will fear no evil, for you
  are with me; your rod and your staff, they
  comfort me. You prepare a table before me in
  the presence of my enemies. You anoint my
  head with oil; my cup overflows. Surely
  goodness and love shall follow me all the
  days of my life, and I will dwell in the house
  of the Lord forever. Amen. - Psalm 23*

- *Our Father in heaven, hallowed be your
  name. Your kingdom come. Your will be
  done, on earth as it is in heaven. Give us
  this day our daily bread. And forgive us our
  sins, as we also have forgiven our debtors.
  And do not bring us to the time of trial, but
  rescue us from the evil one. - Matthew 6:9–
  13 (NRSV)*

- *Father, hallowed be your name. Your
  kingdom come. Give us each day our daily*

*bread. And forgive us our sins, for we ourselves forgive everyone indebted to us. And do not bring us to the time of trial. - Luke 11:2–4 (NRSV)*

- *In the name of God, Jesus Christ, The Great Brotherhood of Light, the Arch Angels Michael, Raphael, Gabriel, Uriel and Ariel, please protect us from the forces of Evil during this session. Let there be nothing but Light surrounding this Board and its participants and let us only communicate with Powers and Entities of The Light. Protect us, protect this circle, the people in this circle and let there only be Light and nothing but Light, Amen.*

- *Dear Spirit, As I light these candles, bless this sacred place.*
  *Let the light of their flames radiate love and protection to all four corners of this room.*
  *I ask at this time that any negative energy be released from this space.*
  *With a bath of white light, I ask that it be cleansed and neutralized.*
  *Turn my dwelling into a sanctuary.*

*May it be the foundation for your teachings and the inspiration for my higher perceptions.*

- *Dear Spirit, As I sit with you now, I open my heart.*
  *I surround myself with the love and light of your protection.*
  *I release any negativity that I have picked up throughout the day so that I speak to the universe with the purity of my soul.*
  *I ask that any energy be given for my absolute good.*
  *Dismiss now all energies that are not of the Highest and Greatest source.*
  *As I bathe in your grace, I will listen to your resounding voice within me.*
  *I will be true to my heart and your gentle guidance.*

## CLOSING PRAYERS/CHANTS FOR OUIJA BOARDS

Ouija closing prayers/chants are performed after moving the planchette to goodbye, flipping it and removing it from the board. Closing prayers can help add closure to the session and help positive energy remain in your circle.

You can use these prayers/chants, or make your own.

After you've said the prayer and thanked the spirits for their time, we always recommend flipping the board and leaving it alone in the room for a while, thus giving any energy remaining in the board enough time to dissipate.

- *"Spirits of light, we appreciate and thank you for your time and wisdom. In the name of Jesus Christ we command all spirits, energy, and entities in this place to return from whence they came. We ask that the Holy Spirit watch over this place and the people in it, cleansing this home with holy light, keeping evil at bay. In Jesus's name we pray. Amen."*

- *"Thank you for the wisdom and insight you have granted us. Thank you, oh Lord for answering our questions, through the beings and Angels of the Light. Protect this house and the people who have been here during our stay in your Realm. In the name of The Light we thank you. Amen."*

- *"Oh Spirit, Thank you for sharing this sacred time with us. We appreciate the flow of energy we have just experienced. We will use it for our highest good. We now close this sacred space and ask that your protection surrounds us wherever we go today."*

## THE OUIJA BOARD DEMON

In an extreme case you could possibly come in contact with dark spirits - that are notoriously identified as demons. You can identify them by name, activity or gut instinct.

The most feared is known as: Zozo "The Ouija Board Demon"
This demon has been known under a few alternative names:

Zozo, Demon z, Zaza, Mama, Oz, Zo, Za, Abacus and Pazuzu.

Many Ouija board users claim that they have come in contact with the demon Zozo. But what are the warning signs and what should you personally do if you feel that you have come in contact with Zozo?

Nobody knows what or who Zozo is. Individuals who have come in contact with Zozo have had extremely negative effects. Some of these effects include:

- Bad luck.
- Depression.
- Thoughts of suicide.
- And in other controversial claims: sexual assault.

Many speculate that the demon could be an incubus/succubus - due to the high accounts of people who have experienced paranormal sexual encounters when in contact with ZoZo.

*Incubus: a male demon believed to have sexual intercourse with sleeping women.*

*Succubus: a female demon believed to have sexual intercourse with sleeping men.*

However Zozo is mostly known as a 'Soul stealer'.

*Soul: the spiritual or immaterial part of a human being/animal, regarded as immortal*

This is according to an early 1900's article where it suggests an individual called: Brook

Kenilworth had her soul stolen by her husband "Zozo" - who was mystic. This could possibly be the origin story of this demon.

It is key to know that even though Zozo is mainly associated with the Ouija Board, many people have reported contact with Zozo by using other forms of spirit communication. There are countless reports where people have made contact with this entity while conducting pendulum sessions, automatic writing, electronic voice phenomena (EVP) and even spirit photography.

*Pendulum contact method: Using a weight hung from a fixed point so that it can swing freely, especially a rod with a weight at the end that regulates the mechanism of a clock – in order to contact entities by them moving it with their spiritual energy*

*Automatic writing method: writing said to be produced by a spiritual, occult, or subconscious agency rather than by the conscious intention of the writer. All you need is a piece of paper and a writing device, rest this onto the paper and allow the spirit to write through you. These sessions have the same opening and closing rules as Ouija.*

*Electronic voice phenomena (EVP): are sounds found on electronic recordings that are interpreted as spirit voices that have been either unintentionally recorded or intentionally requested and recorded.*

*Spirit photography method: Spirit photography is a type of photography whose primary attempt is to capture images of ghosts and other spiritual entities - especially in ghost hunting and has a strong history dating back to the late 19th century – various things can be spotted in these images like:*

- *Faces/body parts (select parts like eyes or arms etc.).*
- *Floating objects*
- *Static/waves around people and objects.*
- *Orbs: a circular artefact on an image, created as a result of flash photography - illuminating a mote of dust or other particle. Some believe this is a spirits energy being captured in the mortal world.*

# Signs that You May be In Contact with Zozo

Below are a few recognized signs that indicate that you may have/are in contact with Zozo during a session. Please be aware there are countless paranormal entities, ghosts and less powerful demons that may emulate the Ouija board demon – Zozo. Here are the most common signs:

- Rapid movements of the planchette in a figure of eight.
- Side to side movements of the planchette (In the shape of a rainbow or arch).
- The planchette spells out one of the demons aliases (ZOZO, ZAZA, MAMA, OZ, ZO, ZA, ABACUS and PAZUZU).
- Feeling uneasy, dizzy or deeply depressed during or after Ouija board session.
- Dark shadow movements around or in the Ouija board area.

# WHAT TO DO iF YOU COME iN CONTACT WiTH ZOZO?

- Don't Panic - darker entities feed off of fear.

- It's advised to close the session ASAP – Please do this in the correct sequence. If you are using the Ouija Board to communicate then move the planchette to Good Bye.

- Like always set boundaries directed at the entity. Before starting any spirit communication it is important to set boundaries with ghosts, entities, demons that you may be communicating with.

- Cleanse/Smudge the area, Ouija Board and participants after your session has closed correctly.

- Do <u>NOT</u> use the same Ouija board again after contact. This board must now be destroyed (instructions on how to do so are in the corresponding chapter).

- Do <u>NOT</u> speak/say his name – this is during the session and after.

# DEMON A-Z

This chapter consists of a list of other demons you might bump into on your paranormal adventures (some are followed by a short description about them- if they have characteristics worth noting down). Keep this book close during your sessions to check if one of these names crop up.

Feel free to add your own notes to this chapter.

## A

**Abacus –** The Ouija board demon. This Demon known by many names but most commonly: Zozo.

**Abaddon/Apollyon –** "The king of an army of locusts" – This demons name in Hebrew is: Abaddon, this then translated into Greek means: "The Destroyer". Derived from Christian demonology.

**Abalam /Paimon –** A demon who stems from Christian demonology.

**Abezethibou –** Demon who is involved with magic.

**Abraxas –** This being was also associated with magic and is said to be the source of the term 'abracadabra'.

**Abyzou –** A female demon from Jewish mythology. Is said to cause miscarriages and infant death.

**Achnor**

**Adramelech –** A demon taken from Assyrian mythology and Christian demonology.

**Aeshma –** Demon of wrath, rage and fury.

**Agaliarept –** A demon taken from Jewish mythology.

**Agnan –** A demon who torments individuals using its appearances and wickedness. Has been spotted especially in Brazil.

**Agrat bat Mahlat / Igrat / Iggeret** – Is responsible for sickness and magic. Taken from Jewish demonology.

**Agares** – A male demon that can cause earthquakes and teaches languages. Taken from Christian demonology.

**Agiel** - A demon taken from Jewish mythology.

**Ahab**– The spirit of Ahab's existence is to cause the destruction of God through ordained authority and the Church. The spirit of Ahab symbolizes the denouncing of authority and advocates responsibility.

**Ahriman/Angra Mainyu / Ahriman** - Is a destructive spirit responsible for deceptive or evil thinking.

**Aim/Haborym** – A spirit of manipulation taken from Christian demonology.

**Aka Manah/Akem Manah/Akoman/Akvan -** Is a demon that causes bad will, bad mind, and bad acts.

**Ala –** A demon from Slavic mythology. This demon is female and causes bad weather. Shown visually in Dragon or Serpent likeness or form.

**Aladon**

**Aleon**

**Alal –** From Chaldean mythology. A sexual demon described to have dark hair, large eyes and a round doll-like complexion.

**Alastor –** A possessing entity brought on by a curse. Taken from Christian demonology.

**Alloces/Allocer –** Taken from Christian demonology. Teaches arts and astrology. Induces divination and mysticism.

**Alu -** This demon is a night creature that has no mouth, lips or ears. Supposedly scares people as they sleep. If you become possessed by Alû it can result in unconsciousness and coma. Taken from Akkadian mythology.

## Amnnra

**Amaymon –** A demon taken from Christian demonology.

**Amdusias -** A demon taken from Christian demonology.

**Amy -** A demon taken from Christian demonology. Amy is a male demon that appears as a flame of fire. He is known to seduce induvials.

**Anamalech –** A demon taken from Assyrian mythology.

**Andhaka –** A demon taken from Hindu mythology.

**Andras -** Appears as a winged angel with the head of an owl or raven. Rides upon a black wolf and wields a bright sword. Taken from Christian demonology.

**Andrealphus -** Described as a Peacock who creates loud noises and teaches astrology plus geometry. He also has the ability to turn any man into a bird. Derived from Christian demonology.

**Andromalius –** Has the power of knowledge. Has the ability to gain information about any object, person, location or physical event. Taken from Christian demonology.

**Antichrist –** In Christian terms is a false messiah and is generally regarded as a figure of evil that will falsely claim to be the Christ.

**Anzu / Zu / Imdugud -** Demon behind Psychics and trying to predict the future. From Sumerian mythology.

**Appolyan/Abaddon –** Is known as 'the king of an army of locusts'.

**Armaros –** From the Book of Enoch. Known in Jewish demonology.

**Aremenia/Al or Hal** - Folklore demon from Iran, Central Asia, and southern parts of Russia.

**Armazad**

**Archon** - Is a name/term used in Gnosticism.

**Asag** – A monstrous demon, very hideous in his appearance from Sumerian demonology.

**Asakku** – Demon who attacks and kills human beings, by inflicting fevers. Well known in Babylonian mythology.

**Asb'el** – Demon taken from Jewish mythology.

**Asclepeion** - Demon of healing.

**Asclepius** - Demons of healing.

**Asmodai/Asmodeus** - The demon of lust and twisting people's sexual desires. Mentioned in Jewish folklore and Christian mythology.

**Astaroth Astarte (Ishtar) -** demon of fertility, sex, love and war. Taken from Christian demonology.

**Asura –** A demon taken from Hindu mythology.

**Azazel /Azaz'el Azazelle /Azariah –** He taught men the art of warfare, making swords, knives and shields. He taught women the art of deception by dressing the body, dying the hair and painting the face. He also revealed to people the secrets of witchcraft and corrupted their manners. Taken from Jewish demonology.

**Azi Dahaka/Dahak:** A demon from Iranian mythology. He steals cattle and brings harm to humans. Represented as a snake-like monster with three heads and six eyes.

# B

**Baal/Bael -** A demon taken from Christian demonology.

**Ba'al-Hamon –** From Ugaritic demonology. Known as: "Ruler of a Crowd or Multitude"). He was a deity of sky and vegetation. Visual depicted as a bearded older man with ram's horns. Ba'al Hammon's female partner was Tanit.

**Babopy –** Demon of abortion or homosexual spirit.

**Bakaneka/Bakeneko –** Demon from Japanese folklore. Refers to spiritual beings/animal spirits with supernatural abilities akin to cats (yōkai), fox (Kitsune) or raccoon dog (tanuki).

**Balam –** Taken from Christian demonology. Depicted as being three-headed. One head is the head of a bull, the second of a man and the third of a ram. He has flaming eyes and the tail of a serpent. He carries a hawk on his fist and rides a strong bear. Other times he is represented as a naked man riding a bear.

**Balberith** – Taken from Jewish demonology. Tempts men to blasphemy and murder.

**Bali Raj/Bali or Māveli** – Taken from Hindu mythology.

**Banshee** – Popular in Irish mythology. Is a female spirit seen as an omen of death and a messenger from the underworld.

**Baphomet** – From Christian folklore. A goat like deity.

**Barbas** – From Christian demonology. The demon of Fear.

**Barbatos** - A demon taken from Christian demonology.

**Barron** - A demon taken from Catholic demonology.

**Bathin/Mathim/Bathym/Marthim** - A demon taken from Christian demonology.

**Beball** – From Christian demonology. Known to be a stupid demon.

**Beelzebub** – From both Jewish demonology and Christian demonology. Beelzebub is another name for the devil, similar to Satan.

**Behemoth** – From Jewish demonology. This name is used or given to any extremely large or powerful entity to describe them.

**Belial /Belisle** – From both Jewish demonology and Christian demonology.

**Beleth** - A demon taken from Christian demonology.

**Belphegor** - A demon taken from Christian demonology.

**Berith/Beherit** – From both Phoenician mythology and Christian demonology.

**Bhairava**

**Bhūta** – Derived from Sanskrit.

**Bifrons -** A demon taken from Christian demonology.

**Boruta –** A demon taken from Slavic mythology.

**Botis –** A demon taken from Christian demonology.

**Buer -** A demon taken from Christian demonology.

**Bukavac –** A demon taken from Slavic mythology.

**Bune -** A demon taken from Christian demonology.

**Bushyasta –** A demon taken from Zoroastrianism.

# C

**Caacrinolaas**

**Cain/Caim/Cali**

# Canacjaza

## Centrioles

**Carabia** – From Christian demonology. This spirit is depicted as appearing as a pentagram star who changes into a man under the conjurer's request.

**Charlie Charlie** – Taken from a modern day folktale. Will appear after the name is chanted over a handmade "yes or no" commination board - using a pencil. Will answer questions you ask it (similar to Ouija).

**Charun** – From Etruscan mythology. A demon from the underworld. He is often portrayed with "Vanth" (a winged goddess who is also from the underworld).

**Chemosh** – Found in the Hebrew Bible.

**Choronzon** – Demon who can destroy the ego.

**Cimejes/Kimaris/Cimeies –** From Christian demonology. A demon that possesses the abilities of locating lost (or hidden) treasures.

**Corson –** A demon taken from Christian demonology.

**Crocell/Procell –** From Christian demonology. Manifests as an angel, with a tendency to speak in dark and mysterious sayings.

**Culsu –** From Etruscan mythology. Culsu is a goddess associated with gateways and death. Appears as a topless winged woman carrying a torch and scissors.

# D

**Daeva –** From Zoroastrianism demonology. A name given to a demon entity with disagreeable characteristics. Known as "wrong gods", "false gods" or "rejected gods".

**Dai Ko Mio -** Reiki master spirit. Its symbol is the Phoenix.

**Dagon –** From Semitic mythology. Fertility god.

**Dajjal –** From Islamic demonology. False god, he is to appear pretending to be the Messiah.

**Dantalion –** From Christian demonology. This demon teaches all arts and sciences. He also knows the thoughts of all people and can change them at his will. He can also cause love.

**Danjal –** From Jewish mythology. A fallen angel.

**Decarabia –** From Christian demonology. He appears as a pentagram star, although he will take the form of a man if the conjurer requests it. He knows the properties/values of all herbs and precious stones and can transform into any type of bird.

**Demiurge –** From Gnosticism. A fallen angel.

**Demogorgon –** From Christian demonology. Demon associated with the underworld. Name is seen as taboo to mention.

**Diablo –** Demon from the self-titled video game. Hasn't been in contact as a 'real' entity but other spirits may use this name to appear more assessable to a younger audience or for comical reasons.

**Div-e Sepid –** From Persian mythology. Is the chieftain of the Persian demons.

**Drekavac –** From Slavic mythology. Is a mythical creature who looks like a dog or fox, but with hind legs similar to a kangaroo.

**Dzoavits –** Form Native American mythology. Was a demon/ogre from Shoshonean mythology that stole the sun and kidnapped children. This entity is associated with volcanism and cannibalism.

# E

**Eldonna-** Incubus and succubus: perverted sexual demons.

**Eligor –** From Christian demonology. He discovers hidden things and knows the future of wars.

**Eisheth –** From Jewish demonology. Woman of Whoredom.

**Eblis –** From Islamic demonology. A fallen angel.

**Ethismus –** From Jewish demonology. Demon of infirmity.

# F

**Falling Stars/Fallen Star/Star –** Name given to demons that fly up towards heaven and overhear God's plans then fall back to Earth. Making them look like shooting stars to humans.

# Fluris

**Focalor –** From Christian demonology. Appears in the form of a man with griffin wings. Kills men by drowning them and overthrows warships.

**Foras/Forcas/Forras –** From Christian demonology. He teaches the virtues of all herbs and precious stones. This entity can also discover treasures and recover lost things.

**Forneus –** From Christian demonology. He is depicted as a great sea monster.

**Furcas/Forcas –** From Christian demonology. Furcas is depicted as a strong old man with white hair and long white beard, who rides a horse while holding a sharp pitch fork. He teaches Philosophy, Astronomy, Rhetoric, Logic, Chiromancy and Pyromancy.

**Furfur –** From Christian demonology. This demon is a liar. Furfur causes love between a man and a woman, creates storms, tempests, thunder and lightning.

## G

**Gaap** – From Christian demonology. This demon has the powers to teach philosophy and liberal arts, make others invisible, make men stupid and carry men between kingdoms.

**Gader'el** – From Jewish demonology. A fallen angel. He taught the art of cosmetics and the use of weapons/killing.

**Gaki** – From Japanese mythology. Name given to entities known as "hungry ghosts".

**Gamigin** – From Christian demonology. Teaches liberal arts.

**Ghoul** – Commonly found in Arabian and several other mythologies. Name given to an evil spirit or phantom, especially ones who rob graves and feed on dead bodies.

**Glasya/Labolas/Caacrinolaas/Caassimolar/C lassyalabolas/**
**Glassia-labolis –** From Christian demonology. He is the author and captain of manslaughter and bloodshed. Tells all things past and to come, knows all sciences, gains the minds and love of friends and foes.

**Gorgon –** Popularised by Greek mythology. Three Gorgon sisters, Stheno, Euryale, and Medusa, had snakes for hair, and that they had the power to turn anyone who looked at them to stone.

**Gremory/Gomory –** From Christian demonology. He has knowledge of all things past, present and future. He is depicted as appearing in the form of a beautiful woman.

**Grigori –** From Jewish demonology. Watcher angel.

**Gualichu –** An evil demon that possesses men.

**Guayota** – From Guanche mythology. Was said to be represented as a black dog and was accompanied by demons (who were also in the form of black dogs).

**Gusion/Gusoin/Gusoyn** – From Christian demonology. Depicted as a baboon. He has knowledge about the past, present and future.

## H

**Haagenti** – From Christian demonology. Depicted as a big bull with the wings of a griffin. Can change into a man under request of the individual who summons him.

**Hat Man** – This demon spirit is the most common seen. Some authors think this is the devil himself.

**Hathor** – From Egyptian Mythology. This entity is usually depicted as a cow goddess with horns. Hathor is an Ancient Egyptian goddess who symbolises joy, feminine love and motherhood.

**Halphas/Malthus –** From Christian demonology. This entity is often depicted in the shape of a stork and ignites war.

**Haures/Flauros/Flavros/Hauras/Havres –** From Christian demonology. Commonly depicted as a horrifying and strong leopard that can change into a man under request of the conjurer. Flauros is supposedly called upon when a mortal wishes to take vengeance on other demons.

**Herodeus –** An entity that is more focused with putting pleasure before knowledge.

**Hon-Sha-Ze-Sho-Nen**

**Horus –** From Egyptian Mythology. Most often depicted as a falcon, or as a man with a falcon head. God of the sky.

**I**

**Ifrit –** From Islamic mythology. Entities that are known for their strength and cunning.

**Incubus** – From Christian demonology, Chaldean mythology and Jewish folklore). These are entities that cause overwhelming sexual urges in the body. Is said to be responsible for sexual dreams, they can manifest also in nightmares. In extreme cases people have reported that these spirits have also engaged in sexual intercourse with them.

**Ipos/Ipes** – From Christian demonology. Commonly depicted with the body of an angel, the head of a lion, the tail of a hare and the feet of a goose.

**Iblis** – From Islamic demonology. Considered as another name for satan.

**Ishtar/Astarte/Isis** – The demon of fertility, love, sex and war.

**Irritum** – From Catholic Christian demonology. This entities name means: "nothingness". Also seen as the spirit of depression.

# J

**Jeqon –** A  fallen angel.

**Jezebel -** Associated with false prophets and lust.

**Jinn –** From Islamic demonology. Are said to be creatures with complete free will. They are made from smokeless fire by Allah (God).

**Jikininki –** From Japanese mythology. They are human-eating spirits. Born from greedy individuals, who are cursed after death to find and consume human flesh.

**Juno Caelestis/Neith -** A war goddess.

# K

**Kabandha/Kabhanda –** From Hindu mythology. A demon (Rakshasa) who is represented as a headless torso.

**Kasadya** – From Jewish demonology. Associated with murder, killing and abortion. A fallen angel.

**Kokb'ael** – From Jewish demonology. A fallen angel.

**Kroni** – Is said to be the first/primary manifestation of evil and shapes into many forms.

**Krampus** – From Germanic-Christian Demonology. Is a horned figure that is said to punish/eat misbehaving children during the Christmas season.

## L

**Labal** – A small, vampiric black demon with whose energy flows from his eyes.

**Landis**

**Lastis Latiangle** - A demon taken from Christian demonology.

**Laxis**

**Legion –** A demon taken from Christian demonology.

**Lechies –** From Slavic demonology. Russian demons that lived in the woods. They had a part human and part goat appearance. They are believed to have kidnapped young women.

**Leonard –** Said to be the "master of the nocturnal orgies of demons". Is an incubus demon.

**Leyak –** From Indonesian mythology. Has the form of flying head.

**Lempo –** From Finnish mythology. An extremely erratic spirit with high energy.

**Leraje/Leraie –** From Christian demonology. This spirit causes battles, fights and disputes.

**Leviathan –** From Jewish demonology and Christian demonology.

**Lodeus**

**Louts –** An aggressive and drunken spirit.

**Lilith –** From Sumerian mythology, Akkadian mythology and Jewish folklore. Lilith is known as a night demon.

**Lucifuge Rofocale –** From Christian demonology. Is said to be the demon in charge of Hell's government (As ordered by Lucifer).

# M

**Makilla –** A creature mixed between a troll, human and demon.

**Malphas –** From Christian demonology. This entity builds houses, high towers and strongholds. However they can destroy buildings/forts of enemies. He accepts kindly any sacrifice offered to him.

**Mammon –** From Christian demonology. A false god referenced in the New Testament.

**Maricha –** From Hindu mythology. Said to be involved in kidnapping and can take the form of animals.

**Marax/Morax/Foraii –** From Christian demonology. This entity teaches Astronomy (other liberal sciences too) and knows the virtues of all herbs and precious stones. He is often depicted as a man with the head of a bull.

**Marbas –** From Christian demonology. Appears in the form of a lion. He brings diseases but also has the power to cure them. He can change men into other beings and shapes. This entity shares his wisdom and teaches/shares his knowledge of mechanical arts and crafts.

**Massah –** A very weak and strange demon.

**Mabley**

**McCoffa**

**Mahamaya**

**Majestic –** Said to be the demon of alternative music (Metal/Rock).

**Marchosias –** A demon taken from Christian demonology.

**Marsuvius –** This entity is depicted as a wolf with gryphon wings and a serpent's tail. Powers include producing fire from his mouth.

**Masih ad-Dajjal/Ad-Dajjal/Dajjal –** A demon taken from Islamic eschatology.

**Mastema –** A demon taken from Jewish demonology.

**Mephistopheles –** From Christian folklore and German folklore. Is a demon that is seen as another version of satan.

**Merihem –** From Christian demonology. Spirits that cause diseases and illness (pestilences).

**Moloch -** From Christian demonology. Associated with idolatry and child sacrifice.

# Muin

**Murmur** – From Christian demonology. Depicted as a soldier riding a Vulture/Griffin.

**Mustafa** – A demon Samurai.

## N

**Naamah** – From Jewish demonology. Is a demon that causes epilepsy in children.

**Naberius/Cerbere/Naberus** – From Christian demonology. This entity appears as a three-headed raven or dog. Can also be depicted as a crow or black crane.

**Naphula** – From Christian demonology. Appears in the form of a lion with Gryphon's Wings. Teaches crafts, philosophy and sciences.

**Necromancer** – Is a term for a person who practices necromancy (practice of communicating with the dead). However some demons refer to themselves as a Necromancer as they may dabble in magic.

**Ninurta** – From Sumerian mythology and Akkadian mythology. This spirit is a solar deity.

**Namtar** – From Sumerian mythology. Considered responsible for diseases and pests.

## O

**Omnicephus Voodoo/Santeria/Kongo/Macumba/Umband a/ Quimbanda/Candomble/Palo** – Demon that goes by many names. Originated from African Cults.

**Onoskelis** - Female demon with a beautiful appearance.

**Oray Lerajie/Leraie/Leraikha/Leraye/Loray** – From Christian demonology. This Entity causes great battles and conflict.

**Orcus –** From Roman mythology and later on in Christian demonology. Was a god of the underworld who punished individuals who broke oaths.

**Orias/Oriax –** From Christian demonology. An entity that is very wise and teaches astrology.

**Ornias -** Is a fallen angel. Has the gift of prophecy, shapeshifting and causing physical pain with its touch.

**Orobas –** From Christian demonology. Described more as an "oracle"(a type of priest/priestess who acts as a medium) rather than a demon.

**Ose -** A demon taken from Christian demonology.

**Ördög –** A demon taken from Hungarian mythology.
**Osiris**

# P

**Paimon –** From Christian demonology. Binds men to the conjurer's will.

## Palmetto

**Pazuzu –** Another name for Zozo (refer to the pervious chapter for more information).

**Peri –** Described as winged-like spirits.

**Perthalus -** A horned demon.

## Petey

## Petula

**Phenex –** From Christian demonology. A kidnapping spirit depicted as a phoenix, which sings beautifully with the voice of a child. This music is said to be extremely dangerous any conjurer must cover their ears and demand the spirit take on a human form to avoid harm.

**Penemue** – From Jewish and Christian demonology. A fallen angel.

**Philo Deus** – A harmful and evil demon.

**Phoenos**

**Pithius** – A lying entity, extremely untrustworthy.

**Pontiff**

**Preta** - A ghoulish demon from Buddhist lore.

**Prostador**

**Pruflas** - From Christian demonology. Causes men to create conflict.

**Puloman** – From Hindu demonology. Name simply means demon.

**Purson/Curson** – From Christian demonology. Depicted as a man with the face of a lion.

**Python –** This entity is known as the spirit of divination. Python empowers crystal ball readers, palm readers and tarot card readers (allowing them to see into the future).

## R

**Rah –** The sun demon.

**Rahab –** From Jewish folklore. Is a mythical sea monster or "demonic angel of the sea" Rahab is also seen as a deity.

**Raim –** Depicted as a crow which can transform into human form. Known as a kidnapping demon.

**Raka –** From Argentina Folk tales. Known for being evil.

**Rakash-** Shapeshifting entity derived from Hebrew.

**Ramael –** A fallen angel.

**Raul/Roul –** Sexual Demon.

**Raum –** From Christian demonology. Spirit of theft and kidnapping.

**Ronove –** From Christian demonology. He harvests souls of humans and animals near death.

**Rusalka –** From Slavic mythology. Known as a water nymph/female spirit.

**Rakshasa –** A demonic being from Hindu mythology.

**Rangda –** From Hinduism. Is the demon queen according to traditional Balinese mythology. Terrifying entity that is said to eat children.

**Ravan –** From Hinduism. Demon who is depicted with ten heads.

**Reaver –** Greek/Roman origins. Magical spirit who has mastered divination.

# S

## Sabnock/ Sab Nac/Sabnac/Sabnach/Sabnack/Sabnacke/ Salmac/Savnock – From Christian demonology. He effects war and wounds from battle.

## Sei-He-Ki – A Guiding spirit.

**Saleos** – From Christian demonology. Causes men to love women and vice versa.

**Samael/Samhel** – From Jewish demonology. A fallen archangel, also known as "The Demon of death".

**Satan** – From Jewish demonology, Christian demonology and Islamic demonology. The most known demon of all. Brings evil and temptation and is known as the deceiver, who leads people astray.

**Salpsan** – Said to be the son of Satan.

**Samurai** – Demons who seek to restructure the world to fit their own desires.

# Schlitz

**Scox/Shax/Chax/Shan/Shass/Shaz –** From Christian demonology. He takes away the sight, hearing and understanding from people.

**Seir –** From Christian demonology. A demon in a goat-like form.

**Semyaz –** From Jewish demonology. A fallen angel.

**Shadow Person (Hat Man) –** Causes terror and feeds off of others fear. The devil himself.

# Shale

**sharu–** Known as "The god who kills with arrows".

**Shedim –** From Jewish folklore. The Hebrew word for demons/false gods.

**Shemal-** Cross-dressing demon/transvestite demon.

**Sitri –** From Christian demonology. Has strong control over relationships.

**Sthenno –** From Greek mythology. Known as the eldest Gorgon. Murderous spirit.

**Stolas/Solas –** From Christian demonology. Teaches astronomy and has extensive knowledge of poisonous plants, herbs. Is known as a poison demon.

**Succubus –** From Sumerian mythology, Akkadian mythology, Jewish folklore and Christian demonology. A succubus is a female demon/supernatural entity that appears in dreams and takes the form of a woman in order to seduce men (mostly through sexual activity). They can appear through spiritual contact - they aren't just limited to dreams.

**Surgat –** From Christian demonology. Is known as a "lock opener".

**Stry**

# T

**Tanit –** A female spirit. Said to be a moon goddess.

**Tar**

**Tjoko-Rei**

**Toumy**

**Tommyknocker –** acts like a poltergeist but is commonly found in tombs and caverns.

# U

**Ukobach –** From Christian demonology. Fire demon.

**Uvall –** From Christian demonology. Has knowledge of the past and present.

# V

**Valac** – From Christian demonology. Gives answers about hidden treasures. Said to appear as a small poor boy with angel wings riding on a two-headed dragon.

**Valfor/Malaphar/Malephar** – From Christian demonology. Called "The Duke of Thieves". This entity tempts people to steal.

**Vapula** – From Christian demonology. Teaches philosophy, mechanics and sciences. Depicted as a griffin-winged lion.

**Vassago** – From Christian demonology. Appears as the angel of light and is a positive demon. Well known murderer and vampire-themed cult leader Rod Ferrell used "Vassago" as his "vampire alias". Rod Ferrell appears occasionally through spiritual communication but will still refer himself as Vassago. Therefore be careful when coming into contact with a spirit who identifies themselves with this name, as they may turn out to be an evil entity.

**Vepar –** From Christian demonology. Watches over the waters and guides ships. Vepar is usually depicted as a mermaid. This spirit can also help people levitate and can cause serious disease (mostly to men at sea).

**Vesuvius**

**Vine –** From Christian demonology. This demon is portrayed as a lion type creature. This entity can bring down walls and build towers.

# W

**Wekufe -** Also known as huecufe, wekufü, watuku, huecufu, huecubo, huecubu, huecuvu, huecuve, huecovoe, giiecubu, güecubo, güecugu, uecuvu, güecufu. Harmful and evil spirit/demon from Mapuche mythology. Extremely deceptive and lies.

**Wendigo –** From Native American Mythology. Also known as windigo, weendigo, windago, windiga, witiko, wihtikow, and manaha. Described as a demonic half-beast. The creature/spirit could either possess characteristics of a human or a monster. Is known to possess or mimic people and voices. Wendigo's are also known for their cannibalistic appetite. Some people have reported to have encountered a wendigo through Ouija in which it impersonated different passed on spirits to mislead members of the circle.

## X

**Xaphan –** From Christian demonology. A fallen angel.

**Xezbeth –** Said to be the demon of lies and legends. This entity will invent false tales and give misleading information.

## Y

**Yemayah –** Originating from Nigeria. An evil female entity. She is described as long-breasted and wears crystal and blue beads.

**Yeqon** – A fallen angel.

**Yeter'el** – A fallen angel.

## Z

**Zagan** – From Christian demonology. A fallen angel.

**Zepar** – From Christian demonology. A fallen angel.

**Ziminiar** – From Christian demonology. Known as "The king of the north".

**Zozo, Zaza** – Known as "The Ouija Board Demon". Please refer to the previous chapter, which is dedicated to this particular demon.

# How to destroy a Ouija Board

After countless research it's been extremely difficult to find a completely safe or recommended way to dispose of an Ouija board. However here are a few methods I've found.

- People usual say "Just burn it." However according to spiritual professionals burning is said to cause more damage - As negative energy/demons are said to dwell in hell which is made of fire.

- It's also believed that you can sell them on and that will pass on anything tied to the board (and you) onwards to the next owner. However, this is deemed as unmoral and a sign of bad luck for you.

- Some have buried their unwanted Ouija boards face down. Making sure that the planchette and the board do not touch each other during (or after) the burial, as that can cause the spirit to come out of the circuit. In a similar way its sometimes recommended you take the Ouija board then break it into seven pieces, sprinkle holy water over these pieces and finally bury them (in peaceful separate areas). I personally believe physically causing harm to the board might provoke negative energy, so I wouldn't advise this myself.

- In extreme cases (like the board moving itself and poltergeist activity following it) then it has been known for people to bring their boards to willing priests/exorcists for cleansing in a holy manner.

- Most say the safest method for disposal is actually not to throw it away at all. You just need to have perspective and make sure that the board was closed down properly during the last session. Make sure you wrap the planchette in any form of cloth (so it doesn't make actual contact with the board). Then place the board in an isolated room (No living spaces/bedrooms) or secure box. Even if you find yourself speaking to a high level demon when the board is closed correctly all bad energy will be eradicated.

THANK YOU FOR SUPPORTING PUMPKIN PUBLICATIONS, I HOPE YOU'RE NOT TOO SPOOKED.

PLEASE LEAVE A REVIEW IF POSSIBLE, AS YOUR FEEDBACK IS MUCH APPRECIATED.

## About The Author

M. Cryptkeeper is a graduated Art student based in the United Kingdom (London/Essex). With a passion for illustration and horror it only made sense for her to start Pumpkin Publications: An indie book company that specializes in Modern horror folk tales and hand drawn colour therapy.

Her quirky style instantly translates into her books creating a truly immersive experience.

95443706R00047

Made in the USA
San Bernardino, CA
16 November 2018